Guilty as Sin:

Uncovering New Evidence of Corruption and How Hillary Clinton and the Democrats Derailed the FBI Investigation

Summary

& Analysis

Summarized By

Easy Input

FREE GIFT SPECIAL REPORT

The Tidiest and Messiest Places on Earth

After reading this summary you may conclude that the Middle East seems like a mess, but we made a special report about the Tidiest and Messiest Places on Earth! This report is a great supplement to that summary that is all about the virtues of being tidy.

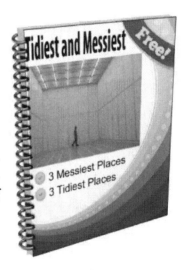

As our **free gift** for being an **EASY INPUT enthusiast** we are happy to give you a special report about the **3 Most Messy** and the **3 Most Tidy** places on Earth.

Learn about everything from **Garbage Island** to Computer-Chip **Clean Rooms** (and, of course, everything in between).

Get your **free copy** at:

http://sixfigureteen.com/messy

ALSO: We will let you know about future Easy Input titles so this is **win-win**! Enjoy your **FREE GIFT** and thank you for being part of the **EASY INPUT** Family!

EASY INPUT

Copyright © 2016 The Six Figure Teen Trust

All rights reserved.

ISBN-10: 1539674142
ISBN-13: 978-1539674146

DISCLAIMERS

- Absolutely nothing in this volume is meant to constitute legal, financial, or medical advice nor are the opinions presented to be considered expert opinions.
- This volume is **NOT** meant to be a replacement for the original book, we believe our summation, key quotes and highlight analysis will increase interest in the complete book and not detract from it.
- In this volume, each detail is presented to the best of our knowledge and understanding of the recent book on the Clinton FBI Investigation. If you think any of our analysis, or review is inaccurate **please email us** and we will correct it and publish an updated edition after we verify it (easyinputbooks@gmail.com).
- Most importantly: absolutely no portion of this summation volume was written in a Starbucks.

CONTENTS

GUILTY AS SIN – *SINGLE PAGE SUMMARY* 7
CHAPTER 1: THE SKY IS FALLING 8
CHAPTER 2: AN ANGEL SHOOTS A CHERUB 10
CHAPTER 3: HER FATAL FLAW 11
CHAPTER 4: KALE SALAD AND A MASSAGE 13
CHAPTER 5: BLINDSIDED 14
CHAPTER 6: BROKEN PROMISES 15
CHAPTER 7: LOVE JOE BIDEN 17
CHAPTER 8: THE SMELL TEST 19
CHAPTER 9: A ONE-EIGHTY 21
CHAPTER 10: COLLISION COURSE 22
CHAPTER 11: Citizen Comey 23
CHAPTER 12: STACKING UP THE EVIDENCE 24
CHAPTER 13: THE CLINTON BRAND 26
CHAPTER 14: PAY TO PLAY 28
CHAPTER 15: THE GENERAL HAS ARRIVED 29
CHAPTER 16: HIGH NOON IN THE OVAL 30
CHAPTER 17: EVEN GOD CAN'T READ THEM 32
CHAPTER 18: CONSPIRACY OF SILENCE 34
CHAPTER 19: MY WORST MISTAKE AS PRESIDENT 35
CHAPTER 20: THE BLUMENTHAL ASCENDANCY 37
CHAPTER 21: TRUMP FORCE ONE 38
CHAPTER 22: CROOKED HILLARY 40
CHAPTER 23: WOULD TRUMP BE WORSE 42
CHAPTER 24: HILLARY'S "VALERIE JARRETT" 44

CHAPTER 25: FIT TO LEAD 46
CHAPTER 26: A TISSUE OF LIES 48
CHAPTER 27: TOO BIG TO FAIL 49
CHAPTER 28: FORT HOOVER 51
CHAPTER 29: A PERFECT STORM OF MISERY 52
CHAPTER 30: FROM THE POLITICAL FRYING PAN TO THE FIRE 53
CHAPTER 31: IN THIS TO THE END 55
Bonus Feature: Critics Analysis 56
FURTHER READING 57
FREE GIFT SPECIAL REPORT 58
FREE GIFT SPECIAL REPORT 60

GUILTY AS SIN – *SINGLE PAGE SUMMARY*

Guilty As Sin goes into detail about a 16-month FBI investigation involving the email scandal of Hillary Clinton. Klein shares the dynamics of Bill and Hillary's rocky relationship and her undying love for her top aide.

In an unusual turn of events President Obama finds himself protecting the person he hates the most in Hillary Clinton. Guilty as sin shows conversation with Obama and how he wanted to get any other possible Democratic nominee to run. Once that failed he endorsed a political enemy.

The relationship of Hillary and her daughter Chelsea has long been debated. This book devotes an entire chapter to the volatile relationship between the two.

Overall this book shares with the reader the great detail it took FBI Director Comey to conclude his 16-month investigation and all the political posturing that went on to ensure that Hillary would walk free.

This is a very hard book to put down.

CHAPTER 1: THE SKY IS FALLING
(SUMMARY & KEY POINTS)

It was July 2015 and Hillary Clinton just learned of the impending FBI investigation for her mishandling of classified e-mails as Secretary of State.

Her temper tantrums in situations like this had grown to legend status as she would repeatedly blow up. Her chief advisor remembers her stating that FBI director, James Comey, would end up like all the other Clinton enemies.

This brash and borderline psychotic behavior has been with Hillary Clinton for years. In 1974 Hillary worked for Bernard Nussbaum, senior member of the House of Representatives Watergate Committee, she blew up on Nussbaum when he had doubts that her boyfriend, Bill Clinton, would one day become the President of the United States.

Nussbaum remembers the profanity-laced tirade he was offered by Hillary. He remembers thinking how could someone that works for me talk to me in such a way? How can anyone speak to a boss so disrespectful over a hypothetical?

Several times she would physically grab the arm of a staffer that had enraged her. Bill would step in and attempt to calm her down and that only enraged her more.

All of this seemed to come to a head when Republicans demanded she give a testimony on her mishandling of the Benghazi attack that took the lives of the U.S. Ambassador and three other Americans.

Hillary Clinton lied to the families telling them the attack was the result of an anti-Islamic video when in reality it was an al-Qaeda-affiliated terrorist group that led the attacks.

For Hillary Clinton any attack on her was from the Republican side of the fence. She never could admit to any wrongdoing on her own part.

Key Points

Secret Service agents have shared that being put on Hillary detail was considered the worst job in the entire Service. It was likened to a form of punishment because of how harsh she treated everyone around her.

CHAPTER 2: AN ANGEL SHOOTS A CHERUB

(SUMMARY & KEY POINTS)

Hillary had famously stated she was a radical feminist that wanted to end the "racist, sexist, capitalist system." She arrived in Little Rock to see Bill Clinton in 1973 looking the part. She wore thick glasses, untidy hair, and no makeup.

Hillary grew up with an abusive father that never made her feel good enough. For instance, if Hillary forgot to put the tube back on the toothpaste he would throw it out the window and make her retrieve it in the snow, barefoot and all.

She boasted, famously, she was named of Sir Edmund Hillary and in reality he was unknown until six years after her birth. She has changed her name several times to go with the group she was trying to get elected by.

Greg Gutfeld, cohost of Fox News' *The Five*, stated that Hillary is "about as likable as elective surgery. Every time she speaks, an angel shoots a cherub."

Key Points

At one point she was married and known solely as Hillary Rodham. When Bill was elected governor of the southern state of Arkansas she became Mrs. Bill Clinton. As her own political ambitions grew she became Hillary Rodham Clinton.

CHAPTER 3: HER FATAL FLAW

(SUMMARY & KEY POINTS)

Literary minds have compared Hillary to Lady Macbeth who became so ambitious that it led to her downfall. She is willing to say anything to any person. For instance she has claimed that all her grandparents were immigrants to the United States, in reality, one grandparent immigrated and the other three are natural born citizens.

She has lied so many times it is becoming difficult to remember specific times. She lied about never sending classified material over her e-mail. It turns out there were more than two thousand documents on her server. Twenty-two of those were marked "special access program," which is higher than top secret.

Hillary Clinton lied when she said she gave no special favors to foreigners that donated to the Clinton Foundation as Secretary of State.

Hillary has been caught with plenty of lies and it shows in polling. Sixty percent of Americans consider her untrustworthy and when Gallup asked Americans what word came to mind when the heard the name Hillary Clinton the majority replied - dishonest.

Key Points

One Clinton Foundation donor was a Canadian businessman that was granted State permission to sell control of 20 percent of American's uranium production to Vladimir Putin. After the sell Bill Clinton was paid $500,000 to come to Russia and give a speech.

CHAPTER 4: KALE SALAD AND A MASSAGE

(SUMMARY & KEY POINTS)

Bill Clinton loved to visit the William J. Clinton Presidential Library and Museum and eat dinner and get foot massages from the interns working the library.

One day he is getting a foot massage discovered the Hillary told some Iowa Democrats that she is on snapchat because it deletes all of her emails.

Key Points

Bill knew that she was publicly messing with the FBI and he had to fix it.

CHAPTER 5: BLINDSIDED

(SUMMARY & KEY POINTS)

Bill brings in one of his closest friends to the Clinton's penthouse terrace trying to figure out how to control the e-mail situation that Hillary was clearly exasperating.

Bill's advisor unveiled several sheets of paper to illustrate how bad this could be for Hillary. These papers included indictments such as:

- Flouting federal laws governing record-keeping requirements
- Failing to preserve emails sent from personal accounts
- Circumventing the Freedom of Information Act
- Instruct her aides to send classified documents on an unprotected server
- Gross negligence of the Espionage Act
- Pretending not to know that Sensitive Compartment Information was classified
- And many more

Key Points

Bill and his advisor devised a plan and Bill noted that he would try but Hillary would do whatever she wanted.

CHAPTER 6: BROKEN PROMISES
(SUMMARY & KEY POINTS)

Bill was scheduled to golf in a foursome that included one of his least favorite people in the world, President Barack Obama. The Clinton's had been learning that it was the White House that leaked the information about the classified e-mail snafu that has plagued much of Hillary's campaign.

The Clintons had always felt that Obama's presidency was just another interregnum between Clinton I and Clinton II.

Obama remained frustrated because he paid off Hillary's 2008 campaign debt and made her Secretary of State and still had the knowledge the Clintons were out to get him.

President Obama, in his own words, felt that if Hillary Clinton won the White House he would be marginalized in his own party and felt he had to find someone to replace her as the nominee.

As Bill was headed to Martha's Vineyard for the golf game he received a phone call from a friend saying that word in Washington was the Obama was working to get Joe Biden's campaign running. He immediately called and told Hillary the news and she threw a flower vase across the hotel room.

The golf game started with Bill asking Obama about his endorsement and Obama said "I'm not endorsing." It proceeded with Bill arguing with Obama about his role in the FBI investigation of the classified e-mails.

One thing was sure, the Obamas and the Clintons feud was growing by the moment.

Key Points

Bill was not surprised to learn the leaks were from the Obama Administration. He felt, for some time, that the president himself would do anything to derail Hillary's presidential bid.

CHAPTER 7: LOVE JOE BIDEN
(SUMMARY & KEY POINTS)

The first week Stephen Colbert hosted the Late Show his production team landed Joe Biden as a guest. Joe stated that he always wondered why you would want a job in the White House if you weren't willing to be who you really were and to say what you really wanted. This was an obvious hit on Hillary Clinton and her perpetual lie train that she couldn't seem to stop.

According to sources Beau Biden's dying wish was that his dad save America from the Clintons and start a bid for the White House himself.

Joe had a concern. His reputation was pristine. He could leave the VP office with his dignity or he could get in the dirt with Hillary and let all the old news surface again.

Hillary had some artillery ready to aim at Joe Biden if he dared come against her:

- He plagiarized speeches and five pages of a report during law school
- He supported a mandatory minimum sentencing for federal crimes that would result in a high African American incarceration rate
- He had been accused of sexual assault
- He did not back the president in the raid that killed Osama bin Laden

Key Points

The sources that released Beau Biden's dying wish stated there was only one person that could have come from and that was Joe Biden. He wanted that information to get out to the public.

CHAPTER 8: THE SMELL TEST
(SUMMARY & KEY POINTS)

President Obama began urging Elizabeth Warren to jump in the race. Hillary had continued her assault on Bernie Sanders, but Warren was different.

Warren was the personification of the new Democratic party that was almost undecipherable from a socialist party. She was supported by several left-wing militant groups such as:

- Black Lives Matter
- Occupy Wall Street
- Service Employees International Union
- The Sierra Club
- Emily's List

Warren, though powerful remained hesitant to join the race because she never wanted to be on the bad side of the Clintons. In reality it became clear that Warren didn't run because of her past records and not because of her fear. She could not pass the smell test.

Key Points

These left-wing militant groups badly wanted Elizabeth Warren to run. Warren remained hesitant.

CHAPTER 9: A ONE-EIGHTY

(SUMMARY & KEY POINTS)

President Obama had been turned down by Biden and Warren and Obama kept waiting for someone new politician to come to the rescue, like him in 2007, they never came.

For a brief moment Obama turned his sights to Bernie Sanders. He was quickly assured that the black vote and middle America would never turn out for him.

After all the analysis Obama quickly realized that any faction at this point would result in the Democratic party losing the election soundly.

He feared:

- Bernie supporters forming a third party
- A democratic collapse if Hillary was removed at the DNC
- A confused party if she was arrested and removed because of the scandal

Key Points

President Obama could not bear endorsing Hillary Clinton. His vanity and self-admiration would never let him. Though it seemed inevitable Obama was taking a hit in his health as he dealt with the idea that Hillary would be his candidate.

CHAPTER 10: COLLISION COURSE
(SUMMARY & KEY POINTS)

Elizabeth Shapiro was one of the prosecutors handling the Clinton email investigation. She was requested to visit the director himself, James Comey.

Comey was getting the feeling that the Justice Department was deviating from an indictment. Truth be told Shapiro had a 20 plus year relationship with the Clintons and had a no indictment mindset the entire time.

As Jim Comey say it the Justice Department was running out of time. The current president was not going to allow his attorney general to indict the presumptive Democratic nominee. Comey realized he was on a collision course with the Attorney General and needed all the support he could get.

Key Points

Mistrust had been growing between the Justice Department and the FBI. This case would cause a collision course.

CHAPTER 11: Citizen Comey

(SUMMARY & KEY POINTS)

Shapiro brings her assistant Marcia Berman to the meeting with Comey. She recognizes this is a battle between the liberal left and the conservative right and wants as much support as she can possibly muster.

Comey found prominence in the 1980s as a United States attorney in New York. He famously prosecuted billionaire Marc Rich that had illegally traded oil with Iran, while Iran held fifty-two Americans hostage. President Clinton offered Marc Rich a full presidential pardon and it is still considered the most condemned act of his political career.

During George W. Bush's tenure Comey, then Deputy Attorney General, strongly opposed the warrantless wiretapping program that Bush put into place of 9/11. This was hailed as a great victory for the Democrats and the reason President Obama placed Comey as FBI Director.

Like many prosecutors Comey is deeply religious. He attends church services several times a week and is the Sunday School teacher at his church.

Key Points

Comey did not realize how supporting Berman was of the Obama administration. She had been an ardent supporter of Obama's 2012 campaign and was a staunch liberal.

When Rich received the presidential pardon that was when Comey realized that politics trump justice. He felt that this case was heading in the same direction.

CHAPTER 12: STACKING UP THE EVIDENCE

(SUMMARY & KEY POINTS)

As the meeting started Shapiro and Berman sat at the Comey conference table. Comey had a team assembled that included: Deputy Director Mark Giuliano, Andrew McCabe, and Jim Rybicki.

Comey started the meeting with a stack of yellow legal pads and asked his assistant to type these up so that he can see how the evidence stacks up to Hillary Clinton.

Comey focused on three particular questions:

1. Was Hillary guilty of gross negligence in the handling of national security secrets?
2. Was Hillary guilty of public corruption by offering foreign governments and businessmen favors in return for donations to the Clinton Foundation?
3. Did Hillary lie to the FBI or conspire to suborn witnesses?

The argumentative discussion lasted until two in the morning as the FBI Director did everything in his power to show that these charges would stick. Shapiro simply was not buying it.

Key Points

One FBI attention stated that the information and evidence in these drafts would never fly with Attorney General Lynch.

CHAPTER 13: THE CLINTON BRAND

(SUMMARY & KEY POINTS)

Bill Clinton received a phone call from an FBI agent asking him to have a meeting with the FBI and a prosecutor to simply clarify something's about his wife's use of an insecure email server. Clinton lost it on this request and said he would never go near an FBI agent at any cost.

Immediately following this exchange Bill called Hillary and berated her for putting him into this position. He blamed her longtime aides Huma Abedin and Cheryl Mills for allowing her to use this email server for classified documents.

Bill was also upset that Hillary's criminal investigation and campaign had caused some celebrity friends, including Leonardo DiCaprio and Pope Francis, to turn down an invitation to the Clinton Foundation's annual gala in New York.

Bill made it clear that he did not have the fire for a presidential campaign. His health made it hard for him and he stated more than once that he didn't have the anger you would need to continue the fight.

What made it even harder for Bill is that he fundamentally disagrees with his wife on several key political issues.

Bill states that Hillary buys all the left-wing crap that she did when she was in college. She has never left her socialist, feminist, ways.

Key Points

After the lengthy phone argument with Hillary, Bill collapsed into bed. He was exhausted. His doctor had already warned him that there was nothing that could be don't to reverse his heart disease. He was convinced he didn't have long to live.

CHAPTER 14: PAY TO PLAY

(SUMMARY & KEY POINTS)

A diplomat was asked by the FBI to speak on the conflict of interest that Hillary had with her role as the Secretary of State while running the Clinton Foundation.

This diplomat was a retired Foreign Service officer that had flown with Hillary on several State Department missions overseas.

This diplomat states that she is a Democrat and a supporter of Hillary for President was always resented that she treated the office of Secretary of State as a part-time job so that she could grow the Clinton Foundation.

After the interview with the FBI this diplomat had decided that the FBI was coming after Hillary Clinton with a vengeance.

Comey had a history with Hillary Clinton. In the 1990s as deputy special counsel to the Senate Whitewater Committee he learned that Hillary Clinton personally mishandled documents and had ordered others to block investigators as they pursued their case.

To Comey this was a case that had been a long time in coming,

Key Points

Clinton always stated that it was ok that she did both jobs because they complemented each other.

CHAPTER 15: THE GENERAL HAS ARRIVED

(SUMMARY & KEY POINTS)

The Capitol Grille is a "manly" eatery in D.C. where the power suits of the FBI and the Justice Department go to argue over cases.

One such argument was over the Hillary Clinton case. Many on both sides of the table admitted that the investigation was going at a snail's pace and would've been concluded already if it had been any other person other than the presumptive Democratic presidential nominee.

Several Justice Department prosecutors that were sympathetic to Clinton's politics but realized that allowed Special Access Program documents to pass through an unsecured server was an appalling use of power.

Many at the table felt that a jury would never convict the Democratic nominee without proof of criminal intent. The challenge to this statement was that Hillary violated Title 18 that prohibited knowingly and willingly making false statements and concealing information. There was no doubt Hillary had violated, criminally, Title 18.

Key Points

Many prosecutors were found saying that they couldn't believe that Hillary didn't know these were classified documents because she had been a Senator, First Lady, and Secretary of State. She knew what classified material looked like from a mile away.

CHAPTER 16: HIGH NOON IN THE OVAL

(SUMMARY & KEY POINTS)

On January 29, 2016 it was revealed to FBI Director Comey that White House spokesman Josh Earnest stated that based on what he knew there was probably not going to be an indictment on Hillary Clinton.

Comey had never shared anything with the White House, in reality it was not any of their business to be briefed on this investigation.

Comey soon discovered the Attorney General Loretta Lynch had been stopping by with a copious amount of documents at the White House on numerous occasions to keep Obama updated on the investigation.

Comey's job was to gather as much information as possible and make a referral to the Justice Department. Ultimately it would be up to the Attorney General to decide whether charges should be pressed.

Comey began to fear that politics, not evidence, would be the chief decider in this case.

It was a great irony that Obama's great enemy, Hillary Clinton, would get a get out of jail free card by him and the only thing that stood in his way was the man he appointed to direct the FBI.

Key Points

These meetings between Lynch and the White House were unethical, therefore, Lynch denied the meetings.

CHAPTER 17: EVEN GOD CAN'T READ THEM

(SUMMARY & KEY POINTS)

The entire investigation of Hillary Clinton was lengthy. It included:

- Ten thousand pages of reports
- About two and a half million words
- The equivalent of four copies of *War and Peace*

The only negative so far was that the cyber department of the FBI had only been able to retrieve a fraction of the 31,000 emails Hillary had wiped clean from her personal server.

Trey Gowdy, chairman of the House Select Committee on Benghazi, made the remark that these emails were deleted and wiped clean so much so that even "God can't read them."

Bryan Pagliano was the IT Specialist for BleachBit. He was able to state that the following countries had hackers that had tried to break into Hillary's private email server:

- China
- Russia
- North Korea
- Iran
- And several other countries

Key Points

Hillary used a company called BleachBit to wipe her server. The IT specialist that helped with this process, Bryan Pagliano, pleaded the Fifth Amendment so that he would not incriminate himself. He was eventually granted immunity in exchange for his testimony.

CHAPTER 18: CONSPIRACY OF SILENCE
(SUMMARY & KEY POINTS)

Seeing the odds continuously being stacked against him Comey contacted John Brennan, director of the CIA, and James Clapper, director of National Intelligence, explaining to them the importance of them standing with the FBI in this crucial time.

As the conspiracy of silence was taking shape it became apparent to Comey that the White House ensured that he was alone in this investigation.

Comey began to see how many normal requests made by the FBI were ignored or denied by the other intelligence agencies in the government. It was obvious that these agencies did not want to be on the wrong side of the Clintons or the White House.

Comey's relationship with Obama had deteriorated to the point that he found the White House trying to move moles over from the Justice Department to the FBI to spy on Comey and his team.

Key Points

Brennan and Clapper assured Comey he would have their unwavering support in this investigation. However, in the end, nothing happened of the sort. It has been called a "conspiracy of silence."

CHAPTER 19: MY WORST MISTAKE AS PRESIDENT

(SUMMARY & KEY POINTS)

Obama, overheard by Valerie Jarrett, was talking about Director Comey saying: "I appointed the son of a bitch. Doesn't he have to do what I say?"

Obama was infuriated because Comey had turned down a presidential request to come to the White House and discuss the Clinton case.

Obama stated that he gave Comey the best job a cop could want and he returned the favor by being a registered Republican and, if he convicts Hillary, handing the election over to the Republicans.

Obama saw through the idea that Clinton would be forgiven and not convicted because she had no criminal intent in the mishandling of her emails.

Meanwhile the hacker Guccifer was imprisoned for hacking into Hillary's emails and was giving lots of interviews to anyone that asked. Obama realized that Comey was giving the ok for this and soon realized he could stop it by ensuring that the Attorney General silence Guccifer. Obama would do anything to keep the American people from thinking about Hillary Clinton and emails.

Key Points

Their relationship deteriorated to the point that Obama stated that giving Comey the job as FBI Director was the worst mistake he made as president.

CHAPTER 20: THE BLUMENTHAL ASCENDANCY

(SUMMARY & KEY POINTS)

Hillary trusted her trop three aides more than she trusted her own husband. She always felt that Bill looked out for Bill. Hillary knew that her top aide Huma Abedin would go to Sing Sing before she would rat her out to the FBI.

As her back was pressed to the wall by the FBI investigations of the Clinton Foundation and the email scandal Hillary turned to Sidney Blumenthal.

Blumenthal was a young journalist on the campaign trail for Bill's gubernatorial race in Arkansas. In the 1990s Blumenthal started making the shift from respected journalist to propagandist by defending the Clintons at almost every turn.

Blumenthal spread fiery rumors about Obama during the 2008 primary campaign. Professor Peter Dreier wrote in May 2008 that he had received an email attacking Obama's character every day for six months and Blumenthal and the Clintons tried to destroy their opponent.

Key Points

Blumenthal has been longed blamed for spinning the Monica Lewinsky scandal into a stalker relationship.

CHAPTER 21: TRUMP FORCE ONE

(SUMMARY & KEY POINTS)

Klein wrote a story on Trump Tower in 1994 that never ran in the magazine, but, it brought the two together multiple times.

In 2012 Klein wrote a piece on Trump that shared his mounting influence in the Republican Party. Trump stated that he only fired people on television and yet people respect and want to hear his political opinions.

From the initial announcement of his candidacy most pundits thought he wouldn't make it through the primary, but if he did Clinton would pulverize him on every single level.

In reality Clinton's "unlikeability" and Trump's brutal honesty have been a storm that has forced Hillary to take Donald seriously.

Klein was invited to fly on the so nicknamed Trump Force One to have some time to interview the presidential nominee.

Trump was flipping through the station on the television to see what media outlets were talking about him. He saw a negative interview on CBS and immediately fired an email to them asking why the let an unchecked person be so defamatory.

Key Points

From 2012 on it became clear that Trump had more aspiration than taking over New York City. Trump wanted the White House.

CHAPTER 22: CROOKED HILLARY

(SUMMARY & KEY POINTS)

A few weeks after that flight Trump contacted Klein asking why the media was fighting his every word and never saying anything about Hillary? Klein felt like Trump had a valid argument.

Bob Woodward of the Washington Post admitted that they had twenty reporters sent to dig up dirt on Trump. When asked how many were sent to dig dirt on Hillary, he couldn't muster an answer.

Most media outlets admitted that the anti-Trump conspiracies were true. The reasoning was that it was ok because he was showing off the worst parts of America.

Michael Goodwin wrote in the New York Times that "the shameful display of naked partisanship by the elite media is unlike anything seen in modern America."

Trump responded to this bias by playing to his nearly 16 million social media followers. He created the following monikers:

- Low energy Jeb
- Little Marco
- Lyin Ted
- Crooked Hillary

Key Points

Hillary responded to the "Crooked Hillary" moniker by reminding the people that Trump attacked minorities and women. She had a game plan to crush Trump.

CHAPTER 23: WOULD TRUMP BE WORSE
(SUMMARY & KEY POINTS)

On June 2, 2016 Hillary unleashed her attack on Donald Trump. It was powerful and it even forced some conservatives to admit it wasn't all untrue.

One of the key aspects of his campaign she attacked was his use of Twitter. She asked the American population what it would look like if Trump had control of America's nuclear weapons when he was angry just like he has control of Twitter when he vents now.

Many Democrats feared that the only way to attack this Republican candidate is something Hillary could not do. With her call to get him a psychiatrist to explain his love of tyrants she showed she had the gall to fight the way this campaign demands.

In 1980 many Republicans started a Dump Reagan campaign and it failed. The #NeverTrump campaign was destined to fail as well.

The Republicans were stuck with an unwanted candidate and they had to endorse him for three reasons:

- Every vote that didn't go to Trump would go to Hillary
- Every non-vote by a Republican was a vote for Hillary
- Every vote for an independent conservative was a vote for Hillary

Key Point

The Twitter and nuclear weapon combination has been a powerful blow to the Trump campaign.

CHAPTER 24: HILLARY'S "VALERIE JARRETT"

(SUMMARY & KEY POINTS)

Huma Abedin shies from the spotlight. She is tough, you have to be to work with Hillary all these years, but doesn't enjoy it when Hillary shows lots of interest in her with others around.

The conversation with a group of friends showed Hillary realized she was surrounded on all sides. Her Benghazi mistakes were catching up to her, the email scandal continued to swirl and she knew the FBI was coming.

To make matters worse Hillary had grown tired of Bernie Sanders. She felt that he had spoiled her well earned nomination party.

This party of private friends of Hillary turned quiet when someone asked her where Bill was and she said she didn't know but he was probably with some….. and let her voice trail off.

As Hillary talks about Bill she begins trying to pull her hair out of her head in a violent attempt to show how "crazy" he makes her. Huma pulls her out of the room and one of the friends remarks that Huma had grown so close to Hillary that it must incense Chelsea.

Chelsea and Hillary have had a remote and somewhat cold relationship. Chelsea, like her mom, is not a warm person. One close friend remarked that the only time the two show emotion is for the camera.

Chelsea has an overinflated view of her political savvy and thinks herself as her mom's Valerie Jarrett. She might have only known the political spotlight but she made a fool of herself in her one attempt to stump for her mom when she started blasting Bernie Sanders relentlessly. The Democratic brass has asked that Chelsea be restrained.

Key Points

Hillary has grown accustomed to Bill's indiscretions as the dark part of his personality. But she is growing tired of his mental lapses as he has blown up at some of her supporter's rallies.

CHAPTER 25: FIT TO LEAD
(SUMMARY & KEY POINTS)

The overwhelming fear in the Clinton camp was that if the Comey investigation didn't get her, her health would.

Conveniently the liberal media has largely chosen not to engage the topic of her health. In fact when a conservative brings up her health, like Trump or Sean Hannity, they are vilified and considered as evil and dishonest.

Since 2005 Hillary has had many fainting spells that continue to mount concern for her well-being as president. Through many medical tests it has been revealed that Hillary has a tendency to form blood clots and to faint.

It has been revealed that some of Hillary's doctors considered performing valve-replacement surgery. The negative fallout it could produce on the political landscape thwarted this idea.

Three months after she announced her candidacy Hillary's doctor wrote a two-page report giving her a clean bill of health. After research it is clear that there are some misleading statements in this report. Upon research these are facts that the opposite was stated in the report:

- She drinks a beer everyday
- She hates yoga
- She has no personal trainer to help her with weight training
- Her vigorous walking was simply strolling around the house

Key Points

Hillary's health concerns are not without warrant. The job of president of the United States of America is the most stressful job in the world. Someone must hold this office in top physical condition.

CHAPTER 26: A TISSUE OF LIES

(SUMMARY & KEY POINTS)

Hillary has been caught with an email to her aide Huma Abedin that states: "I don't want any risk of the personal being accessible." This is the chief email link that shows that Hillary is guilty as sin.

On May 25, 2016 the ombudsman for the State Department issued a seventy-nine-page report that showed her trail of lies.

Hillary did not comply with a host of federal laws and rules on handling her emails.

There are a host of statements made by Hillary that were either a lie or irrelevant. Effectively a majority of her defense in this case sits on a tissue of lies or is completely irrelevant.

It was deemed irrelevant for classified documents not to be marked classified. As previously stated someone as close to classified material for as long as Hillary has been should be able to recognize these documents from a mile away.

Key Points

At this point 60% of Americans already believed Hillary was an untrustworthy liar. The ombudsman's report solidified the suspicion Americans have had.

CHAPTER 27: TOO BIG TO FAIL
(SUMMARY & KEY POINTS)

When the president publicly endorsed Hillary Clinton he sent two messages. The first was the he wanted no part of Trump in the White House and the second was that she had zero chance of indictment.

Many close to the situation stated thoughts like this:

- **She certainly sent classified documents on an unprotected server**
- **She participated in pay-to-play by giving preferential treatments to non-American entities through the Clinton Foundation while she was Secretary of State**
- **She did suborn witnesses since her aides forgot most of what happened when she was Secretary of State**
- **She would never pay for her crimes because President Obama simply didn't want her too**

At the time of the endorsement it was wildly thought that even if Comey and the FBI issued a referral and urged the Attorney General to pursue the case she simply would not.

There was one person that did not have the view of the all powerful president and that was the president himself. With six months to go as president he now subscribes to the view Truman had in the presidency where he stated that Eisenhower would have a hard time because no one listens to the president like they do a commanding officer in the military.

Key Points

While the president continued to fight Comey he finally went to Lynch, just weeks before the Democratic National Convention, and told her it was her responsibility to protect Hillary at all costs.

CHAPTER 28: FORT HOOVER

(SUMMARY & KEY POINTS)

Comey was feeling the pressure from all sides. As Independence Day came around he and his top officials were still piecing together their investigation into the email scandal.

Comey still received no help from the CIA, NSA, or DIA. He needed the tech side of the government to chip in and all were afraid she would win the presidency anyway and they would be immediately fired.

Helped finally arrived in the form of Julian Assange, founder of WikiLeaks. He promised to unleash a hoard of emails that would convict Hillary on the spot.

Key Points

Comey was running out of time and he might not have enough time for Assange to come up with what he promised.

CHAPTER 29: A PERFECT STORM OF MISERY

(SUMMARY & KEY POINTS)

The mass-murder of 49 people in a gay nightclub in Orlando, Florida proved to be just what Hillary needed to fight Comey.

Blumenthal and her other minions used the FBI's fumbling of Omar Mateen as a reason why he should back off Hillary's investigation. To Hillary's team Comey was wasting valuable anti-terrorist resources at the FBI to come after someone that had no criminal intent.

As the threats continued Hillary began to privately buckle under pressure. Her fainting and coughing spats were happening frequently in the private eye and her doctor had chosen to monitor her daily.

Through all of the hoopla in this case Hillary never once allowed negative talk to come into her point of view. Her closest allies never once remembered her saying "If I am indicted" or anything similar.

Key Points

Hillary started gaining more support from the academic circles that helped in the confusing rhetoric the Clintons had engaged in for some time. They would state that she acted criminally but did not break the law. This only led to more confusing aspect of this case.

CHAPTER 30: FROM THE POLITICAL FRYING PAN TO THE FIRE

(SUMMARY & KEY POINTS)

By the time July 5th rolled around it was obvious that Hillary Clinton was guilty. The only question was whether or not she was prosecutable.

To Comey this investigation was strange and should never be considered a normal investigation. The reason for this is cited:

- Bill Clinton barged onto Attorney General Lynch's plane, Comey's boss, making it appear it was a rigged investigation
- The president of the United States caused the intelligence community to shun the FBI
- Democrats accused Comey of campaigning against Clinton
- Democrats called Comey Captain Queeg to show he was unhinged
- Republicans wanted Hillary's head on a platter
- Conservatives think the whole thing is rigged

No matter what Comey seemed to be in a lose-lose scenario.

Through great anguish Comey chose not to recommend an indictment against Hillary Clinton. Comey never chose to explain why he didn't recommend an indictment.

Key Points

Initially Comey had regret by not indicting Clinton. In the end he rationed that it was a prudent idea. He harmed her politically and showed she could not be trusted.

CHAPTER 31: IN THIS TO THE END
(SUMMARY & KEY POINTS)

After the non-indictment Clinton surged ahead in the polls and started destroying Donald Trump. The momentum gained was stopped suddenly by a bombshell shared by the Associated Press.

The AP reported that more than half the non-governmental people Hillary met with when she was secretary of state gave money to the Clinton Foundation.

This bombshell was huge for a few reasons:

1. The AP investigation carries a lot of weight because it isn't tied to a political party
2. It revealed James Comey was unaware of the extent of Hillary's personal meetings
3. It created a firestorm in the FBI's ongoing investigation of the Clinton Foundation's pay-to-play scheme

Key Points

In the end the Clinton's do not believe that this case will be taken seriously by the voting public and Hillary is end this to win it, at all costs.

Bonus Feature: Critics Analysis

At Easy Input we always enjoy summarizing bestsellers for those with not enough time read all the bestsellers coming out or just want to get a taste before deciding to get a full version (which is always much more expensive).

Edward Klein goes into great detail explaining the process, from all sides, of the FBI's investigation into the email scandal by then Secretary of State Hillary Clinton. From insider interviews all the way to candid reports from hackers in prison Klein spares no rock unturned in discovering whether or not Hillary is guilty as sin.

We think this verified Amazon user said it best in his review of this title:

I knew the Obama's and Clintons hated each other but not how deep it went. Obama also hates Comey ("worst mistake of his Presidency") and initially wanted FBI to recommend indictment... But he couldn't convince Biden to run. Thus the flip and reluctant phony endorsement for Hillary. Now BO is campaigning for her as if he's running for a third term.

On Amazon.com there are very few reviews listed for anything under five stars. This is a **quality** book!

EASY INPUT

FURTHER READING

Are you ready to quickly absorb the main points and highlights of the next best seller? Check out great summaries from these great brands,

Slim Reader and Slim Reads:

- If you liked this news guide you will LOVE our summary the latest Legends & Lies release. **LEGENDS & LIES: The Patriots**, pulls back the curtains and reveals what about the founders was fact and what was fiction; check out our summary here:
  http://amzn.com/B01HORJIZE

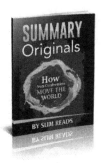

- Looking for inspiration? Check out ***Summary: Originals: How Non-Conformists Move the World | Summary & Highlights with BONUS Action Plan*** is a great read, but it is a LONG book. We have already read it and summarized it for you so pick up a copy and enjoy:
  http://amzn.com/B01DMVEQ12

- Got a taste for **Geo-Politics?** What's really going on in the Middle East? Check out ***Summary: And Then All Hell Broke Loose***. Get the summary today:
  http://amzn.com/B01C7HE4VE

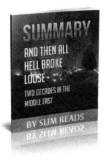

FREE GIFT SPECIAL REPORT
10 Little-Known Facts Even Potterheads Don't Know

Pop quiz hot shot! You think you know EVERYTHING about the Harry Potter series and its amazing rise in worldwide fandom? THINK AGAIN! I'm sure you know your Dumbledores from your Longbottoms but it is time to push your fandom to the next level (that's right, level 9 and 3/4)!

As our **free gift** for being an **EASY INPUT** enthusiast we are happy to give you a special report about the **10 Little-Known Facts Even Potterheads Don't Know**.

Don't let Voldemort keep you from getting this awesome report!

Get your **free copy** at:

http://sixfigureteen.com/potter

ALSO: We will let you know about future Easy Input titles so this is **win-win**! Enjoy your **FREE GIFT** and thank you for being part of the **EASY INPUT** Family!

FREE GIFT SPECIAL REPORT

The 10 Strange Deaths of Vladimir Putin

This election year, a major part of **Trump's foreign policy** message is that he will be able to work together with the Russian head-of-state Vladimir Putin, but what kind of man is Mr. Putin?

As our **free gift** for being an **EASY INPUT** enthusiast we are happy to give you a special report about some of the mysterious and strange deaths that have befallen Mr. Putin's enemies.

Plane crashes, multiple stab wounds and radioactive sushi are just a few of the misfortunes that have befallen those who opposed the Russian President.

Get your free copy at:

http://sixfigureteen.com/putin

ALSO: We will let you know about future Easy Input titles so this is win-win! Enjoy your FREE GIFT and thank you for being part of the EASY INPUT Family!

FREE GIFT SPECIAL REPORT
The Tidiest and Messiest Places on Earth

We made a special report about the Tidiest and Messiest Places on Earth! This report is a great supplement to that summary that is all about the virtues of being tidy.

As our **free gift** for being an **EASY INPUT** enthusiast we are happy to give you a special report about the **3 Most Messy** and the **3 Most Tidy** places on Earth.

Learn about everything from **Garbage Island** to Computer-Chip **Clean Rooms** (and, of course, everything in between).

Get your **free copy** at:

http://sixfigureteen.com/messy

ALSO: We will let you know about future Easy Input titles so this is **win-win**! Enjoy your **FREE GIFT** and thank you for being part of the **EASY INPUT** Family!

Made in the USA
Lexington, KY
17 November 2016